Francis Hutcheson

Selected Philosophical Writings

Edited and Introduced
By John McHugh

LIBRARY OF
SCOTTISH
PHILOSOPHY

IMPRINT ACADEMIC

Published in the UK by Imprint Academic
PO Box 200, Exeter EX5 5YX, UK

Distributed in the USA by
Ingram Book Company,
One Ingram Blvd., La Vergne, TN 37086, USA

ISBN 9781845401603

A CIP catalogue record for this book is available from the
British Library and US Library of Congress

Full series details:

www.imprint-academic.com/losp

Contents

Series Editor's Note

The principal purpose of volumes in this series is not to provide scholars with accurate editions, but to make the writings of Scottish philosophers accessible to a new generation of modern readers in an attractively produced and competitively priced format. In accordance with this purpose, certain changes have been made to the original texts:

- Spelling and punctuation have been modernized.
- In some cases the selections have been given new titles.
- Some original footnotes and references have not been included.
- Some extracts have been shortened from their original length.
- Quotations from Greek have been transliterated, and passages in languages other than English translated, or omitted altogether.

Care has been taken to ensure that in no instance do these amendments truncate the argument or alter the meaning intended by the original author. For readers who want to consult the original texts, full bibliographical details are provided for each extract.

The Library of Scottish Philosophy was originally an initiative of the Centre for the Study of Scottish Philosophy at the University of Aberdeen. The first six volumes, published in 2004, were commissioned with financial support from the Carnegie Trust for the Universities of Scotland. In 2006 the CSSP moved to Princeton where it became one of three research centers within the Special Collections of Princeton Theological Seminary Library, and with the Seminary's financial support more volumes have been published.

Selections from Francis Hutcheson is the sixteenth volume in the series and has been prepared for publication by Alexander Peterson and Jeremiah Barker, to whom a special debt of gratitude is owed.

Acknowledgements

The CSSP gratefully acknowledges financial support from the Carnegie Trust and Princeton Theological Seminary, the enthusiasm and excellent service of the publisher Imprint Academic, and the permission of the University of Aberdeen Special Collections and Libraries to use the engraving of the Faculty of Advocates (1829) as the logo for the series.

Gordon Graham,
Princeton, March 2014

Editor's Acknowledgements

This anthology would not have been possible without the hard work of Jeremiah Barker and Alex Peterson, who turned a pile of facsimiles of Hutcheson's 18th-century texts into the manuscript for the book you are about to read. Also making essential contributions were Noah Bradtke-Litwack, Moriah Ellenbogen, Kristin Edwards, and Christina Hambleton. The same goes for Graham Horswell and the staff at Imprint Academic.

I would like to thank Gordon Graham for providing me with the wonderful opportunity to work on this anthology. I would also like to thank Denison University for funding my trip to the February 2012 Center for the Study of Scottish Philosophy conference at which I had the good fortune to meet Gordon.

Lastly, I would like to thank Aaron Garrett for introducing me to the work of the great Francis Hutcheson.

John McHugh

Introduction

Hutcheson's Life

Francis Hutcheson was born in 1694 into a community of Scots Presbyterian transplants to the Ulster province of Northern Ireland.[1] In 1711, he enrolled at the University of Glasgow. After six years of study, he returned to Ireland to follow in his father's and grandfather's footsteps by becoming a minister. However, unlike his father (and presumably his grandfather, who died in 1711), Hutcheson favored what was then called 'New Light' Presbyterianism, which de-emphasized certain central 'Old Light' doctrines like original sin, defended a relatively optimistic conception of the human condition, and maintained a generally tolerant attitude towards things non-orthodox.[2]

Almost immediately upon his return to Ireland, Hutcheson was invited to run a new 'Dissenting Academy' in Dublin (such schools were established for members of Protestant sects, like Presbyterianism, that 'dissented' from the tenets of the official Church of England). While in

---

[1] This biographical sketch draws upon: Leechman, William, 'Preface' to Hutcheson's *A System of Moral Philosophy, in Three Books* (London: A. Millar, 1755); Scott, W.R., *Francis Hutcheson, His Life, Teaching and Position in the History and Philosophy* (New York: Kelley, 1966); Mautner, Thomas, 'Introduction', *Francis Hutcheson on Human Nature:* Reflections on Our Common Systems of Morality *and* On the Social Nature of Man (Cambridge: Cambridge UP, 1993); and Garrett, Aaron, 'Introduction', to Hutcheson's *An Essay on the Nature and Conduct of the Passions and Affections: With Illustrations on the Moral Sense* (Indianapolis: Liberty Fund, 2002).

[2] For more on Hutcheson's theological context, see Mautner, ibid., 8–14.

Dublin, he became friends with the liberal-thinking Lord Viscount Robert Molesworth (1656–1725). Association with Molesworth and his circle of similarly-minded friends undoubtedly nourished the New Light tendencies already present in Hutcheson's thinking. Perhaps the most significant contribution that Molesworth made to Hutcheson's intellectual development was to encourage him to study the writings of Anthony Ashley-Cooper, 3rd Earl of Shaftesbury (1671–1713). Shaftesbury's attempt to ground morality directly in human nature instead of in divine law had a dramatic impact on Hutcheson's own philosophy, which he introduced to the public through four brief treatises he composed and published during this period.

The first two were published together in 1725 as *An Inquiry into the Original of Our Ideas of Beauty and Virtue*; the second two were published together in 1728 as *An Essay on the Nature and Conduct of the Passions and Affections, with Illustrations on the Moral Sense*. Around this time, he also composed and published in the *Dublin Journal* two series of essays, the first attacking Thomas Hobbes' (1588–1679) attempt to explain the phenomenon of laughter in purely egoistic terms and the second attacking Bernard Mandeville's (1670–1733) argument that the economic prosperity of a nation requires widespread vice among its citizens. Additionally, while in Dublin, Hutcheson might have written or at least started writing, in Latin and thus primarily for the use of his students, *A Compend of Logic*, *A Synopsis of Metaphysics*, and *A Short Introduction to Moral Philosophy*. Precise composition dates for these texts are unknown; the latter two were both eventually published in 1742, while the first was published posthumously in 1756.

The reputation boost Hutcheson received from the writings he published while in Dublin surely contributed to the University of Glasgow's 1730 decision to offer him the position of Professor of Moral Philosophy, which was left vacant after the death of his former teacher, Gershom Carmichael (1672–1729). Hutcheson accepted the position and held it until he died in 1746. While at Glasgow, he completed a manuscript of *A System of Moral Philosophy*, which was published in 1755 by his son Francis and his student-then-colleague William Leechman (1706–1785).

Working with another colleague, James Moor (1712–1779), Hutcheson also completed and published an English-from-ancient-Greek translation of Marcus Aurelius' *Meditations*. The rest (perhaps most) of his energy went into fulfilling his professorial duties. (Hutcheson indicates in his correspondence that he had little time for writing while at Glasgow. With the exception of the translation, most of the literary work he did there, including that on the *System*, further developed ideas already laid out in his Dublin writings and/or presented in his lectures.)

Leechman's biographical preface to the *System* provides a vivid, first-hand account of Hutcheson's character both as a teacher and a human being. We learn from Leechman that Hutcheson aimed at morally inspiring his students as much as, if not more than, he did at improving their grasp of the abstract arguments and positions he taught them in theology, ethics, jurisprudence, and political philosophy. As the selections in this anthology show, Hutcheson's writing tends to be careful and rigorous. But in his lectures, which he delivered in English rather than in the customarily-used Latin,[3] Hutcheson was often willing to sacrifice technical precision for rhetorical force and practical application (xxxiv). Leechman reports that Hutcheson's descriptions of the virtuous life were so engaging that 'students advanced in years and knowledge, chused to attend his lectures on Moral Philosophy, for four, five, or six years together, still finding fresh entertainment, though the subject was in the main the same every season' (xxxiii–iv). Yet he did not merely moralize. He also inculcated such an 'ardor for knowledge' and 'spirit of inquiry' in his students that their casual conversations often 'turned with great keenness upon subjects of learning and taste' (xxxvii).

It appears that Hutcheson also inspired by personal example. According to Leechman, Hutcheson was 'distinguished thro' his whole life' by 'a singular warmth of affection and disinterestedness of temper', traits that manifested themselves in his practice of waiving fees for and pro-

---

3   See Scott, ibid., 62–3.

viding financial assistance to students in need (ii; xxvi). His
'public spirit' made him enthusiastic about 'every thing that
could contribute to the improvement of human life'; thus, he
'took great delight in planning... practicable... not airy and
romantic... schemes for rectifying something amiss, or
improving something already right, in the different orders
and ranks of mankind' (xxvii). And he was simply good
company, due in no small part to his total lack of even a
justifiable level of arrogance:

> A remarkable vivacity of thought and expression, a per-
> petual flow of cheerfulness and goodwill, and a visible air of
> inward happiness, made him the life and genius of society,
> and spread an enlivening influence everywhere around him.
> He was gay and pleasant, full of mirth and raillery, familiar
> and communicative to the last degree, and utterly free from
> all stateliness or affectation. No symptoms of vanity or self-
> conceit appeared in him. He sought not after fame, nor had
> he any vain complacency in the unsought possession of it.
> While he we was visibly superior to others about him, he
> was the only one that was quite insensible of it. His own
> talents and endowments were not the objects on which his
> thoughts were employed: he was always carried away from
> attending to himself, by the exercise of kind affections, zeal
> for some public generous designs, or keen enquiries after
> truth. This was such an acknowledged part of his character,
> that even those who were least disposed to think well of
> him, never insinuated that he was proud or vain... (xxviii–
> ix)

In short, Hutcheson seems to have been a kind, able, and
pleasant man. Echoing Leechman's account with elegant
succinctness, Adam Smith (1723-1790), Hutcheson's student
and eventual replacement at Glasgow, simply deemed him,
'the never to be forgotten'.[4]

Unfortunately, Smith's words have proven to be less than
entirely correct. Hutcheson is not widely read or even widely
known today, despite the fact that his work profoundly
influenced presently canonical moral philosophers like
Smith, David Hume (1711-1776), and Immanuel Kant (1724–

---

[4]   Letter 274 from *Correspondence of Adam Smith*, Ed. E.C. Mossner and
I.S. Ross (Indianapolis: Liberty Press, 1987).

1804). By gathering together some of his most essential writings, this anthology aims at bringing Hutcheson's philosophy into the foreground for readers who have not yet had the opportunity to engage with it directly. With this goal in mind, the rest of this editorial introduction provides: 1) a contextualized overview of Hutcheson's thought; 2) a narrative summary of the anthology's selections; 3) a list of questions to which Hutcheson's views give rise; and 4) a brief bibliography of scholarship on Hutcheson.

Hutcheson's Thought in Context

Hutcheson shared the interest that many philosophers of his day had in human nature. But he thought that his contemporaries were focusing too much on the question of how human beings can acquire knowledge and not enough on the more important, because more practical, question of what makes human beings happy. What was especially needed, he argued, was a thorough study of the various pleasures human beings experience.

We obviously enjoy both physical pleasure and the act of thinking about it. But, Hutcheson points out, we also experience pleasures that do not seem to be either essentially physical or directly derived from ones that are. For example, we experience pleasure when we listen to music and witness intentional acts of kindness. Unlike pleasures that are physical or directly derived therefrom, these pleasures are not explicable by reference to the five 'external' senses alone. Yet like the pleasures that are physical or directly derived therefrom, these pleasures are experienced passively, with no input from our wills. In this respect, they are sensory in nature. Thus, Hutcheson argues, we must recognize, in addition to the five external senses, distinct senses of beauty and morals; he also argues that other kinds of irreducible, non-physical pleasures force us to recognize the existence of distinct senses of sympathy, honor, grandeur, novelty, and dignity. After comparing all the different kinds of pleasures we can experience, Hutcheson concludes that our true happiness lies in the enjoyment of the non-physical or 'internal' ones, especially those of the moral sense, which has a natural authority over the rest of our faculties. (He also draws some political implications from his analysis of human happiness, but these are best left aside until after we have worked through some of the details of his arguments.)

We can best appreciate the distinctiveness of Hutcheson's moral-sense-centered theory of human nature by considering the place it inhabited in his intellectual context. As anyone who has taken an undergraduate course on early modern philosophy knows, there was a debate going on in the period between 'empiricists', who rejected both the notion that the human mind has any ideas innately built into it and the possibility of arriving at any substantive knowledge about the world independently from experience, and 'rationalists', who accepted both the former notion and the latter possibility. By adopting John Locke's (1632–1704) theory of mind, which grounds all our ideas in experience, Hutcheson aligned himself with the former. But he thought that, when it came to morality, many empiricists accepted a false dichotomy between the position that human beings have innate moral ideas and the position that we gain moral ideas solely through the empirical realization that moral behavior best satisfies our selfish interests. Hutcheson saw a non-egoistic middle position: human beings have an innate capacity — *i.e.* a sense faculty — to acquire moral ideas in experience, though without reflection upon their own interests.

In defending the latter aspect of this position — that our moral ideas are not derived from reflection upon our own interests — Hutcheson had two main opponents. The first was the egoistic theory of human psychology that could be traced all the way back to Epicurus (341–270) but had been recently returned to prominence by Hobbes and Mandeville. The other was the theological doctrine, typical of Old Light Presbyterianism, that, given humanity's corruptness, morality necessarily requires the concept of a law backed by divine sanctions. Hutcheson argued that both views are factually incorrect in reducing all moral feeling to concern for self-interest; experience shows that human beings *do* feel sincerely disinterested moral sentiments. He also argued that both views have negative practical consequences. The picture they paint of our neighbors reinforces our prejudices and hostilities, and the picture they paint of ourselves reinforces our selfishness.

Hutcheson's main opponent in defending the former aspect of his position — that human beings have an innate moral sense — were philosophers like Samuel Clarke (1675–1729) and William Wollaston (1659–1724), who thought that *reason*, not a moral sense, must be the faculty we use to make moral distinctions. Hutcheson argued that unlike his own view, this one cannot explain the intrinsic *concern* that is an essential component of moral judgment.

Hutcheson insisted that these apparently unique responses to his contemporaries merely harken back to ancient thinkers like Plato, Aristotle, Cicero, and Marcus Aurelius. Following Shaftesbury, Hutcheson basically endorsed the classical idea that human nature contains within it the resources both to recognize and enact moral goodness.[5] Yet he clearly did not just regurgitate the ideas of his predecessors. None of the ancients employed the concept of a moral sense. And while Shaftesbury did, it is not nearly as fully developed in his work as it is in Hutcheson's. Furthermore, neither Shaftesbury nor the ancients Hutcheson cites aimed as he did at synthesizing the classical ideal with a Christian-flavored, benevolence-based ethic. To see better what Hutcheson's balance between archaism and innovation looks like, let's turn to the anthology's selections.

A Narrative of the Anthology's Selections

Most of the selections in the anthology are taken from the four Dublin treatises. Since Hutcheson revised these works several times each and reused tweaked versions of some of their ideas and arguments in both the *Short Introduction* and *System*, there is scholarly interest in the question of how his thinking developed over time. But new readers of Hutcheson do not have to worry too much about these changes, as few if any of them are fundamental.

---

[5]   Thus, the subtitle to the first edition of the first two treatises includes the lines, 'in which the principles of the late Earl of Shaftesbury are Explained and Defended, against the Author of the *Fable of the Bees* [Bernard Mandeville]: and the Ideas of Moral Good and Evil are established, according to the sentiments of the Antient Moralists'.

1. The Sense of Beauty

The anthology begins with the first treatise, *Of Beauty, Order, Harmony, Design*. In Section I, Hutcheson provides several arguments establishing the existence of the sense of beauty (or, the 'internal sense') by showing that we cannot explain aesthetic pleasure by reference to the external senses alone: sharp external senses do not imply good aesthetic taste; objects like mathematical theorems, which are not grasped by the external senses, can provide aesthetic pleasure; and perfect knowledge of an object's externally sensible features, like its dimensions, does not alone generate aesthetic pleasure. In preparation for his discussion of morality, Hutcheson also argues that aesthetic pleasure cannot be explained in terms of reflections upon one's own interest.

In Sections II and III, Hutcheson turns his attention away from the perceiver's experience of beauty and towards the quality of beauty itself. However, we must be careful regarding how we understand what Hutcheson means by the 'objectivity' of this quality. For Hutcheson, beauty is a quality belonging to beautiful objects only in the sense that these objects possess a *power* to produce the experience of beauty in us. This view classifies beauty as a 'secondary' quality, like sound, as opposed to a 'primary' quality, like motion and extension. Certain objectively-describable, perceiver-independent movements in the air have the power to produce the experience of sound in a perceiver, but, strictly speaking, there is no *sound* without a perceiver. Similarly, certain objectively-describable, perceiver-independent properties of objects have the power to produce the experience of beauty in a perceiver, but, strictly speaking, there is no *beauty* without a perceiver.

Hutcheson argues that the 'original or absolute' objectively-describable, perceiver-independent quality causing our experience of beauty is 'uniformity amidst variety'. This quality is present in a wide range of beautiful objects, including the cosmos, organisms, musical harmonies, works of architecture, and theorems in mathematics, science, and philosophy. (Section IV, which is not included in the anthology, covers the 'relative or comparative' beauty we experience in imitative arts like poetry, as well as in nature, when we think of it as an expression of a divine intention.

Hutcheson's distinction between 'original or absolute' and 'relative or comparative' beauty refers only to the mental process through which we experience beauty, not to the metaphysical status of these qualities. Beauty is 'relative or comparative' rather than 'absolute or original' when our experience of it requires the perception of a relationship between the beautiful object and something else.)

One implication of Hutcheson's metaphysics of beauty is that our experience of beauty does not tell us anything about the world itself beyond how it affects us. In the digressive but important Section V, Hutcheson argues that, for this reason, our experience of beauty cannot alone generate an inference about the nature of the world's cause. However, the fact that the world itself objectively possesses uniformity amidst variety implies that it must be the product of intelligent design; Hutcheson contends that the odds against such orderliness and regularity are just too great for their existence to be an accident. As he will make clearer in Section VIII, once we infer the existence of an intelligent designer, we can treat the aesthetic pleasure we take in this being's design to be evidence of its benevolence towards us.

Hutcheson's next task is to show that the sense of beauty he has identified is both universal and natural. In Section VI, he argues for the former claim by showing that aesthetic disagreements do not provide evidence that people have different senses of beauty. These disagreements, he observes, have mainly to do with *how* beautiful something is, not with whether or not it *is* beautiful; at bottom, everyone agrees in preferring uniformity amidst variety to chaos and disorder. Furthermore, he argues, our views about degrees of beauty often derive from features of human psychology that have nothing to do with the sense of beauty; for example, we tend to think our own culture produces the best art because we naturally grow attached to familiar things. In Section VI, Hutcheson argues that the sense of beauty is natural, not a product of personal experience or social conditioning. He maintains that custom, education, and example can impact aesthetic judgment by enhancing our skill in noticing uniformity amidst variety and by generating association-based prejudices and preferences. But while such forces can shape and direct our natural sense of beauty in these ways, they could never give it to us in the first place; to think otherwise, Hutcheson argues, would be like thinking that a blind person could be trained to see.

Hutcheson closes the first treatise with some reflections upon the relationship between the sense of beauty and practical life. In Section VIII, he investigates how the sense of beauty impacts actual human behavior. He argues that beauty is far more important for our happiness than is physical pleasure; we see this, he contends, when we consider what really motivates our pursuit of wealth and power. Hutcheson also investigates the aesthetic sense's final cause or purpose, which he understands in terms of our creator's intentions. He argues that God must have made it so that our sense of beauty matches up with the structure of the natural world in order to help us navigate life. Imperfect beings like us need the world to be relatively predictable and rule-governed, and it is all the better for us if we naturally *enjoy* discovering and systematically organizing our discoveries of these rules.

2. The Nature of Laughter

Serving as an apt transition to the second treatise, *An Inquiry Concerning the Original of our Ideas of Virtue and Moral Good*, the next selections in the anthology are taken from two groups of articles Hutcheson published in the *Dublin Journal*.

The first selection is from a series of articles attacking the Hobbesian position that laughter results only from a sense of one's own superiority over its object. Unsurprisingly, Hutcheson denies Hobbes' association of humor with vanity and cruelty. Hutcheson's own view, which is reminiscent of his thesis that the sense of beauty responds to uniformity amidst variety, is that laughter most often arises when we observe essentially contrary ideas, like dignity and meanness, grouped together. He also argues that, when used properly, joking around serves the positive purposes of strengthening social bonds and gently exposing character flaws for the sake of correcting them. The second selection is from a series of articles attacking Mandeville's argument that a nation's prosperity rests upon vicious luxury and intemperance in its populace; readers of this selection should keep in mind Hutcheson's observation regarding the connection between the sense of beauty and the pursuit of wealth.

3. *The Moral Sense*

The arguments of the second treatise build upon those of the first in that the existence of a non-socially-constructed, disinterested sense of morality that provides us with a kind of happiness far surpassing anything the physical senses can provide becomes easier to accept once we have accepted the existence of a sense of beauty with the same characteristics. Of course, the inverse is also true, but Hutcheson seems to have thought it less controversial to start with the sense of beauty instead of the sense of morals. As mentioned above, Hutcheson was taking a side in a lively debate about the nature of morality. Thus, in the introduction to the second treatise, he sets up his own argument by distinguishing between an egoistic position that grounds morality in self-interest and a non-egoistic position that grounds morality in disinterested pleasure. Employing a crucial distinction between the perspectives of the spectator and the agent, Hutcheson announces his plan to defend his own version of the non-egoistic account of moral *approval*, but while making clearer than its other proponents had that moral *motivation* is also sincerely disinterested, in that it aims at someone else's good, not at the pleasure of moral self-approval.

In Section I, Hutcheson undertakes the first half of this plan by arguing for the existence of a distinct moral sense. He establishes the moral sense by attacking, in various ways, the egoist's attempt to reduce the pleasure we experience in appreciating virtue to the pleasure we experience in appreciating something because it furthers our interests. Hutcheson invites us to consider the difference between our reaction to someone who helps us for business reasons and our reaction to someone who helps us to the exact same degree but without any self-interested incentives. He also takes on the egoist's attempt to explain in terms of interest our approval of people whose actions do not personally benefit us. The egoist argues that such approval must derive from our consciousness of the fact that *all* virtue at least indirectly serves our interests insofar as it promotes public goods we enjoy, like peace and social stability. Hutcheson responds with several common examples of approval that cannot be explained like this. Are we really thinking about our own interests when we approve of a long-dead historical figure's virtue? What about when we approve of an enemy's virtue, which might even enhance this person's ability to cause us trouble? Hutcheson argues that these and other examples show that we naturally feel approval whenever we perceive virtue, regardless of whether or not this virtue benefits us. Of course, we *can* have the (often true) thought that others' virtue is good for our interests and then applaud and even encourage it for this selfish reason. But the possibility or even prevalence of this kind of approval does not show that there is not a distinct, disinterested, specifically moral kind. And given how automatic it is, the best way to account for this latter kind of approval, Hutcheson concludes, is by positing the existence of a moral sense.

In Section II, Hutcheson turns his attention to that which wins the moral sense's approval. He seems to think that virtue is a secondary quality in the same way he thought beauty is, but this is a matter of scholarly dispute. Regardless of its metaphysical status, the object of the moral sense's approval is disinterested benevolence, which Hutcheson now attempts to prove is real. Mirroring the arguments of the last section, he attacks common egoistic reductions of apparently other-directed motives to underlying self-concern. For example, in response to the argument that all benevolence can be reduced to fear of divine punishment, Hutcheson points out that there are plenty of benevolent people who never or rarely think about God; further, he asks why we would think that God would benevolently reward our benevolence if we think that all rational beings act solely for their own advantage. Hutcheson also attacks the subtler view that when we assist people in need, our goal is only to remove the pain of compassion we feel at the sight of their predicaments. If this were our only goal, he argues, we would *almost never* help others, as turning away is almost always a much more efficient way of alleviating our own sympathetic distress. However, perhaps Hutcheson's strongest arguments for the existence of disinterested benevolence turn on a simple question: other things being equal — meaning, removing any personal stake you might have in the matter—would you prefer to see another human being helped, harmed, or totally unaffected? It just seems plausible that most of us would choose the first.

Section III provides a detailed account of how the moral sense works. Hutcheson's attention in this selection to the consequences of actions might suggest that he is a utilitarian; he even anticipates the utilitarian slogan: 'that action is best, which procures the greatest happiness for the greatest numbers.' However, in contrast with the utilitarian, Hutcheson believes that the consequences of actions are morally important only insofar as they are external signs of an agent's benevolence. This point should be kept in mind especially when reading his set of quasi-mathematical 'axioms' for 'computing' the morality of individual actions. These axioms express a few crucial intuitions about moral judgment, none of which are utilitarian in nature. One is that the presence of self-love in an agent's set of motives detracts from the moral value of the agent's action, regardless of how good its consequences are. Another is that moral evaluation must take into account an agent's abilities; for Hutcheson, all agents who maximize their benevolent *efforts* are capable of achieving 'perfect virtue'.

Two other key ideas about the operation of the moral sense emerge from this section. The first is that the moral sense approves more strongly of our benevolence the wider the circle of people (and sentient beings in general) towards whom it is expressed is. The second is that since disinterested malice, the true inverse of disinterested benevolence, is extremely rare, the object of the moral sense's disapproval is usually excessively weak benevolence, which Hutcheson thinks is the standard source of selfish, negligent, and prejudiced behavior. Notice that this way of explaining vicious behavior suggests that benevolence is morally expected to win out in cases of internal conflict; this feature of Hutcheson's moral psychology plays a major role in his account of moral agency, which is filled out by subsequent selections. Also notice that this account of vice implies that morality requires not just an unwillingness to hurt others but also some level of active concern for their welfare. Thus, Hutcheson owes us some discussion of the baseline level of benevolence requisite for mere moral innocence; passages from *Illustrations on the Moral Sense* dealing with this question constitute the next selection in the anthology.

The remaining selections from the second treatise come from Sections IV and V. The former grapples with the question of how there can be both a natural, universal moral sense and a 'vast diversity in moral principles, in various nations, and ages'. As he did regarding the sense of beauty, Hutcheson argues that this diversity is superficial. Everyone everywhere morally approves of benevolence, but the benevolence of which they approve can be directed in different ways by differing conceptions of happiness, religious beliefs, and prejudices regarding who deserves benevolence. But factors like these cannot create or fundamentally alter the moral sense, which remains natural and attuned to benevolence. The selection from Section V points to the existence of a natural sense of honor, which, Hutcheson argues against Mandeville, presupposes and thus cannot be the origin of the moral sense. (Sections VI and VII respectively cover the practical implications of Hutcheson's moral sense doctrine and its ability to accommodate concepts usually associated with natural law theory; these topics are dealt with to greater effect in passages from the third treatise, the *System*, and the *Short Introduction*, included later in the anthology.)

4. The Passions and the Moral Life

Hutcheson packaged his third and fourth treatises together as *An Essay on the Nature and Conduct of the Passions and Affections, with Illustrations on the Moral Sense.* He wrote these texts partly as responses to three objections he received upon the release of the first two treatises. Thus, the *Essay* opens with a response to John Clarke of Hull,[6] who was dissatisfied with Hutcheson's second treatise arguments for the existence of disinterested desires; the *Illustrations* opens with a response to Gilbert Burnet (1690–1726), who argued that moral distinctions must be rooted in reason and not a moral sense,

---

[6]   It appears that little is known about this John Clarke's life, including his exact birth and death dates.

since we can and must consult reason to decide if we should trust the moral sense's evaluations; and the *Illustrations* closes with a response to an unidentified correspondent who worried that piety played far too small a role in Hutcheson's account of virtue.

The third treatise response to Clarke of Hull occurs within the context of a more exhaustive account of the emotional, non-rational side of human nature than the first two treatises provide. Hutcheson starts the account with an overview of the various senses, which give rise to our desires and aversions by indicating what pleases and what pains us. After differentiating desires in terms of their self- and other-directedness, he further develops several of his second treatise arguments for the existence of the latter. Among these arguments is a more fully developed response to the view, espoused by Clarke of Hull, that a desire for others' happiness is really only a desire for our own because it is a desire for the pleasure we feel upon seeing them happy. Hutcheson argues that these two kinds of desire must be different. Since the latter kind of desire aims at the pleasing, general feeling of a desire being satisfied, it necessarily *presupposes* the existence of a distinct, specific desire, like one of the first kind, that aims at something other than its own satisfaction. Thus, the issue remains whether or not experience provides evidence of irreducible other-directed desires of the first kind. As we have seen, Hutcheson believes that it does.

In the selections from Section II, Hutcheson moves from sensations and desires to affections and passions. He uses the term 'affection' very broadly, but in his most technical usage, it refers to the feelings we have when we anticipate or remember objects of sensation or the events that give rise to it. These feelings can include, but do not have to be, desires (Hutcheson points out that customary usage reserves the term 'affection' for feelings like joy and sorrow instead of for desires and aversions). 'Passions', for Hutcheson, are like affections but are so violent that they inhibit our ability to deliberate rationally. So depending upon whether or not they are connected with a passion, self- and other-directed desires can be calm or violent. Violent self- or other-directed desires usually aim at particular things, while calm self- or other-directed desires tend to be more general. General, calm self-directed desires aim at what we think is our long-term, rationally-considered interest. General, calm other-directed desires aim at what we think is others' long-term, rationally-considered interest; these desires can possess varying degrees of generality, in that they can aim at wider and wider circles of others, all the way out to the entire system of sentient beings.

Once he has laid out this basic framework for the emotional, non-rational side of human nature, Hutcheson uses it to offer some practical advice. In Stoic fashion, he recommends cultivating the calm over the violent desires. Calmness is in our interest because it allows for reflection upon the consequences of our actions. Calmness also tends to secure the approval of the moral sense; as mentioned above, the moral sense favors more generally-directed public desires, which tend to be calmer the more general they are. However, Hutcheson must qualify his general recommendation of calmness. To be completely calm would mean to have only pure desires, which are accompanied by neither passions nor additional affections. But human beings need these extra feelings because their limited intellectual faculties alone cannot be trusted to tell them when to satisfy their necessary desires; to compensate for the force these extra feelings contribute to physical desires, extra feelings are also added to non-physical desires. Thus, since we are unavoidably passionate and affectionate to some degree, our aim should not be complete Stoic calmness but an internal *balance* of feelings.

The first step in explaining how to achieve the self-regulation necessary to achieve this balance is to explain how and to what extent we even *can* control our desires, affections, and passions. In Section IV (the anthology skips over Section III, which catalogs the different affections and passions), Hutcheson argues that we can only regulate our desires, passions, and affections indirectly, by regulating the opinions we have regarding their objects. These opinions can be based upon what our senses naturally tell us is good or bad or they can be based upon customary prejudices and unnatural associations of 'foreign' ideas with the estimations of our senses. For example, we might, as a result of associating the ability to enjoy beauty with economic status, think that the enjoyment of beauty requires ownership of beautiful objects; or we might overestimate the value of certain personality traits because we associate them with celebrities; or we might tend to overlook certain kinds of vicious behavior simply because we are used to seeing it. Hutcheson believes that if we live on the basis of such associations, we are bound to become unhappy because they do not match up with what naturally pleases us and thus disrupt our natural balance. But when they have become habitual, realizing their unnaturalness alone is not enough to break them. We also must change our surroundings and lifestyles. To stick with the just-used examples: we must start getting our aesthetic pleasure from costless and essentially public objects, like wild nature; or we must stop reading the gossip column; or we must start hanging around people of true quality, who consistently demonstrate sincere concern for the interest of the entire public.

Of course, Hutcheson's advice (which I have merely glossed over here) rests upon his conviction that the natural senses provide us with evaluations that can never be totally corrupted, no matter how habitually ingrained our comparatively fleeting associations become. Thus, the fundamental aim of Hutcheson's practical philosophy is to reorient our value judgments so that they reflect what the true core of human nature tells us. But since even our most natural desires and attachments can pull us in different directions, his next task is to explain how we should integrate them. He takes on this task in the next selection, which substitutes a chapter from the *System* for the corresponding one in the third treatise. Foreshadowing John Stuart Mill (1806–1873), Hutcheson argues that if we take into account not only the intensity and duration but also the 'dignity' or quality of the pleasures provided by the various senses, we will see that we are happiest when the pleasure of being moral is our dominant concern.

This argument might give the impression that Hutcheson is, after all, some kind of egoist, who ultimately recommends being moral only on the grounds that doing so will best satisfy the calm general desire for one's own happiness. But, as we see in the next selections (also from the *System*), he offers another argument in favor of the moral life that does not lend itself as easily to this interpretation. He begins by admitting that there may be times when calm self-interest and our most morally approvable desire, calm universal benevolence, come into conflict. Developing a position that was assuredly impacted by his reading of Joseph Butler (1692–1752) and was latent in the first two treatises, Hutcheson argues that the moral sense has natural authority to serve as an 'umpire' in this conflict. His evidence for this claim is partly based on the experience of deliberation, in which moral considerations do indeed present themselves as authoritative. He also appeals to the experience of judging others. We always approve of those who sacrifice their interests for moral reasons and never approve of those who make the opposite trade.

So Hutcheson offers at least two different kinds of arguments in favor of a life in which moral concerns regulate all other ones. One involves a modern-sounding appeal to the superior pleasures of social and moral activity. The other involves an old-fashioned use of teleology, according to which our nature just is such that the moral sense must be in charge for us to function properly as human beings. It is an open question as to whether this argument is egoistic and, if so, whether it is so in the same sense as the first might be.

5. *The Moral Life and God*

Hutcheson also provides a third argument. Closely related to the second one, this argument buttresses the natural authority of the moral sense with considerations regarding the ultimate source of this natural authority. If God designed us so that the moral sense has natural authority, then disruptions of the balance established by the authority of the moral sense constitute disobedience and, more importantly, ingratitude and thus a condemnable lack of benevolence to God. To the extent that it recommends avoiding moral self-hatred, this argument might also be, in some sense, egoistic. It emerges from the next selection, taken from the final section of the third treatise, in which Hutcheson argues that reflection upon the overall goodness of the human condition must generate belief in a benevolent deity; this belief strengthens both our reasons for being moral and our confidence that morality and personal happiness coincide.

Clearly, Hutcheson believed that religious belief and morality are closely linked. Yet, as the next selection shows, he did not believe that morality requires every action to be motivated by love of and obedience to the deity. In Section VI of the fourth treatise, which responds to the unnamed objector mentioned above, Hutcheson argues that those ignorant of God's existence can be morally good, provided that they are sufficiently benevolent. But regardless of their actual beliefs, they must not be prejudiced against evidence in favor of a good god's existence, as such prejudice implies a lack of benevolence; if they truly loved humankind, they would desperately *want* there to be a good god and thus would be receptive to any evidence for the existence of one. And while those who do believe in a good god should love this god most of all, morality does not require that this love dominate their every intention; to be morally good, their actions still must be motivated by benevolence towards their beneficiaries.

6. *Reason's Role in Morality*

As we have seen, the primary target of Hutcheson's moral theory is the egoist, who argues that we only act from concern for our own private interest and only approve of others insofar as we see their actions as conducive to this interest. In the fourth treatise, *Illustrations on the Moral Sense*, he takes on a secondary target, the rationalist, who also rejects egoism but grounds moral motivation and approval in reason rather than in benevolence and a moral sense. The first section responds to Gilbert Burnet's arguments for this view. (Sections II and III, not included in the anthology, respond to the versions of this view respectively espoused by Clarke and Wollaston.) Since this view identifies morally good actions with 'reasonable' ones, Hutcheson starts by analyzing the concept of a reasonable action. He argues that because reason is the faculty that allows us to distinguish truth from falsity, actions can only be reasonable in the sense that we are either lead to perform them or to approve of them because we perceive some truth about them. In the former case, an 'exciting' truth or reason to perform an action might be that it best promotes the public good. In the latter case, a 'justifying' truth or reason for an action might be that it evidences benevolence. But neither action nor approval will occur *at all* unless we first *care* about these truths or reasons. And even if Burnet can explain why we care about these truths or reasons in the first place, he must also explain why we *prefer* actions describable in terms of them to actions describable in terms of truths about what, for example, harms the public or evidences malice. Foreshadowing Hume, Hutcheson argues that these basic evaluative attitudes can only be explained via non-rational aspects of human nature, like sensation and emotion. Thus, he concludes that a view like his is necessarily presupposed by any reason-based moral theory.

But, Burnet worried, how do we know if our moral sense is making accurate moral evaluations? Hutcheson's response is to reject the question. He argues that just as we have no conception of, for example, 'true' or 'real' color to which we can appeal in abstraction from the sense of sight, we have no conception of 'true' or 'real' virtue to which we can appeal in abstraction from the moral sense. As Hutcheson argues in the next selection, Section IV of the fourth treatise, reason can help us correct sensations by referring them to standard conditions of perception, such as those in which the relevant faculty is not affected by disorders like jaundice or prejudice. In the specific case of moral sensation, reason can also help us determine whether the actions of which we approve truly evidence benevolence. Additionally, reason can help us see if an action we are about to perform will truly promote the public good. But in all these cases, reason is only operating in a purely instrumental capacity.

One might also worry that we diminish the merit of virtue by grounding it in an instinct rather than in reason. But, in Section V, Hutcheson argues that since all activity must start from affections and desires, meritorious activity must do so too. Foreshadowing Hume again, Hutcheson supposes that we mistakenly believe that virtue must be rooted in reason because the experience of calm universal benevolence resembles the experience of passionless reasoning. But they must be different because the former can motivate action on its own, while the latter cannot.